Change Your Beliefs To Change Your Life

A Guide To Life Transformation

Nikki Sheikh

© *CHANGE YOUR BELIEFS TO CHANGE YOUR LIFE*
Nikki Sheikh
1st Edition

Publication Date: September 2023
Price: ₹183 | $ 15
ISBN: *978-93-5847-213-4*
Published by:
Adhyyan Books
Office No. 125,
Opposite Vivanta by Taj,
DDA SFS. Pocket-1, Dwarka,
Sec-22, New Delhi-110077
Website: http://adhyyanbooks.com
E-mail: contact@adhyyanbooks.com

Printed at: Repro Printers, Delhi

Contents

INTRODUCTION

The Elephant's Lesson

In India, elephant keepers have a practice of tying up baby elephants to large tree stumps. When these elephants are still small, they are unable to move the stumps. However, as they grow and become stronger, they reach a point where they can effortlessly move these massive chunks of wood. Interestingly, despite their newfound physical ability, the elephants continue to believe that they are incapable of moving the stumps. As we hear this story, many of us feel sympathy for the elephants, realizing that their perception of reality is disconnected from their actual capability to move the stumps. Imagine if I were to tell you that our beliefs work in same way: the beliefs we hold can become self-imposed limitations, hindering us from reaching our full potential.

Soaring kites

In a distant land, nestled amidst rolling hills and lush meadows, there thrived a community known for its unique practice involving soaring kites. Every year, the villagers would gather to construct intricate kites adorned with vibrant colors and delicate patterns. These kites, when flown, would create a mesmerizing dance against the backdrop of the clear blue sky.

There lived a revered elder, Old Man, who was known to have a remarkable bond with the kites. He could fly them with astonishing grace, guiding them through swift turns and daring maneuvers. The villagers marveled at his skill and believed that he possessed a secret technique passed down from generations.

One day, a curious young boy approached Old Man and asked, "How do you control the kites so effortlessly? Is there a hidden trick?"

Old Man smiled and beckoned the boy to follow him.Through winding paths, he led the young boy to a secluded glade, his hand pointing upwards to a majestic eagle riding the currents. "Witness this," he urged, "observe how the eagle commands the sky."

As they watched, young boy noticed that the eagle's flight was not controlled by any strings or mechanisms. It soared with freedom, swerving and diving as it pleased. Old Man explained that the eagle's flight was guided by its instinct and the power within its wings.

"Much like the eagle," Old Man continued, "we humans also have an innate power within us – the power of belief. Just like those kites in the sky, our beliefs can either lift us to great heights or hold us back. our beliefs are like those strings. When we believe in our limitations, we bind ourselves to them, unable to reach our true potential".

And so, this tale reminds us that like those kites and elephants, our beliefs can either hinder us or set us free. By recognizing the beliefs that hold us back and embracing the ones that empower us, we can soar to new heights and uncover the boundless potential within us.

the beliefs we hold in our own lives that act as constraints. These beliefs are responsible for the current state of our lives, which may fall short of our aspirations. Our beliefs, whether conscious or subconscious, play a significant role in shaping our perceptions and actions.

In this book I have discussed the process of belief transformation, shedding light on the profound impact beliefs have on our lives and how they are affecting our reality, our emotions, happiness, our experiences and what strategies we can use to change them in a way that they better serve us not hinder us.

Concepts of Bias, Belief Systems, and Lies

Belief System

Belief systems, are simply our beliefs about the world around us. They are formed through our experiences, upbringing, and cultural influences. We often accept these beliefs without questioning them, and over time, they become deeply ingrained in our minds. However, just because we believe something to be true does not mean it actually is.

There are two primary reasons why people often struggle with life. First, they don't know how to control their thoughts and emotions. Second, they don't know what is true or not. These two factors can make it challenging to navigate through life successfully.

It's essential to understand that just because you love a lie or believe it to be true doesn't make it accurate or truthful. We often become so attached to our beliefs that we are willing to defend them at all costs, even if they are false.

The Zen philosophy suggests that rigorous self-examination can lead us to question our beliefs and uncover the truth. By critically analyzing our beliefs and seeking out alternative perspectives, we can discover the flaws in our thinking and challenge our biases.

Lies are often used to perpetuate belief systems that are not based on facts. We may cling to lies because they are comfortable, familiar, or reinforce our existing beliefs. However, no matter how much we are in love with a lie, it does not make it true.

The key to overcoming this challenge is to learn how to challenge and counter our beliefs. When we fail to question our beliefs, we are living in a state of delusion, which means we are under an illusion. We may believe something to be true, but it's not.

Disillusionment is the process of removing illusions or false beliefs. It can be challenging to confront our biases and beliefs, but doing so is essential to uncovering the truth. Disillusionment can be an uncomfortable experience, but it is also liberating. When we let go of false beliefs, we can free ourselves from the constraints of our belief systems and embrace new perspectives.

Disillusionment is often perceived as a negative experience, but it's important to recognize that it's actually the removal of illusions. When we remove these illusions, we can see things more clearly and make better decisions.

Imagine a student who used to believe that intelligence and abilities were fixed traits, and that failure reflected their inherent limitations. They often avoided challenging tasks and gravitated towards subjects where they felt comfortable.

However, after learning about the concept of a growth mindset—the idea that abilities can be developed through effort and learning—they began to question their beliefs about their own potential. They realized that challenges and setbacks were opportunities for growth and learning.

This change in belief led them to approach their education with renewed determination. They started taking on more challenging subjects, actively seeking out feedback, and persisting through difficulties. Their grades improved, but more importantly, their confidence and enthusiasm for learning grew.

Their journey highlighted the power of embracing challenges and learning from failures, encouraging a more positive and proactive approach to education for themselves and those around them.

VALUES AND BELIEFS - CHOOSING THE RIGHT ONES

THE VALUES AND BELIEFS we hold are essential because they determine the actions we take in our lives. Examining them is critical because, for the most part, we are programmed to believe and act in certain ways without examining them first. Therefore, it's essential to question if our values and beliefs align with the person we want to become.

We can do this through self-exploration, identifying the values and beliefs we hold and questioning whether they are right for us. This process allows us to take control of our lives and make choices based on our authentic selves. We can keep the values and beliefs that serve us well and discard the ones that do not.

For example, consider an individual who values time with their family but also desires financial stability. The two values may be in conflict, leading to a life decision on how to balance both. It is essential to examine and choose the right belief in this scenario to live a fulfilling life. It's natural to feel like we are doing it wrong, but that feeling often comes from societal or familial expectations rather than personal beliefs.

There are various areas to examine, such as beliefs around money, family, honesty, hard work, trust, honor, and the nature of man. Examining these values and beliefs is crucial because they will determine our perception of what we deserve. We often hold erroneous beliefs about what we deserve, leading to disappointment or unrealistic expectations.

Our values and beliefs are integral to our identity and play a crucial role in shaping our thoughts, actions, and perceptions of the world. Examining them is important to living a fulfilling life that aligns with our authentic selves.

Consider the example of someone who values honesty above all else. They may find themselves in a situation where they are tempted to lie, but their commitment to honesty as a core value would prevent them from doing so. Similarly, someone who believes in the power of hard work may push themselves to achieve their goals and overcome obstacles.

However, sometimes our values and beliefs can hold us back or cause us to act in ways that do not serve us. For instance, someone who has been taught to prioritize financial stability may feel trapped in a job they dislike, even if it does not align with their true passions and interests. Examining our values and beliefs can help us identify those that may be limiting us and work to change them.

One way to examine our values and beliefs is through self-exploration and questioning. We can ask ourselves questions such as:

"What are the core values that I cherish the most, and what is the significance behind them?"

“Are there any beliefs or values that I hold that might be hindering me in some way?”

"Am I acting out of habit or societal pressure, or are my actions consistent with my fundamental values and beliefs?"

Through this process of examination, we can identify the values and beliefs that are truly important to us and discard those that do not serve us. This allows us to live a more authentic and fulfilling life, in alignment with our true selves.

Ultimately, this process of examining and selecting our values and beliefs can lead us to enlightenment. By shedding beliefs and values that no longer serve us, we can discover our true purpose and live a life that is truly meaningful and fulfilling.

Through this process, we can free our minds and live authentically. It's important to understand that enlightenment is not about becoming a genius. Instead, it is about realizing what isn't true and taking that out of our repertoire. By discarding what is not true, we can live in alignment with our values and beliefs and become "enlightened" or "lightened."

The Nature of Beliefs

In order to manifest our desires into reality, it is crucial that the frequency of our desires aligns precisely with the frequency of our beliefs. A tangible example of this principle can be seen when contemplating the goal of financial abundance. Suppose someone desires to attain financial prosperity but consistently holds a belief that money is scarce and difficult to come by. In this scenario, their desired financial abundance cannot manifest. To attract financial abundance, it is necessary for both the desire for wealth and a positive belief in the abundance of opportunities and resources to coexist. Only then can the manifestation occur, as our thoughts and actions generate a resonance that attracts the desired outcome.

Consider someone who's in pursuit of a deep and supportive romantic relationship. However, if they're carrying the belief that they don't deserve love, it's like they're unintentionally putting up barriers. It's akin to broadcasting, "Don't approach, I'm not meant for affection." To make their desire for a truly fulfilling relationship a reality, a change needs to happen. They must cultivate a genuine sense of self-worth and embrace the idea that they are indeed deserving of the love they seek. Once they shift their perspective from doubting their worthiness to recognizing it, they create a pathway for the right kind of love to enter their life. Transforming their belief becomes a catalyst that enables them to attract the authentic and loving relationship they've been yearning for.

Imagine someone who's striving to excel in their career and climb the ladder of success. Yet, they often grapple with self-doubt, believing they lack the skills and competence required to achieve their goals. This self-perceived inadequacy becomes a stumbling block, leading them to hesitate when opportunities arise, or even to avoid applying for higher positions altogether.

In order for them to realize their aspirations of career advancement, a shift in their belief system is essential. They need to transition from seeing themselves as incapable to recognizing their potential for growth and achievement. By cultivating self-confidence and adopting a positive belief in their ability to learn and adapt, they cav pave the way for success. With this new perspective, they're more likely to seize opportunities, take on challenges, and strive for excellence in their professional journey. Changing their belief becomes a driving force that empowers them to reach new heights and fulfill their career ambitions.

By challenging the way we think about beliefs and reality, we embark on a journey of personal growth, unleashing our untapped potential and crafting lives that align with our deepest desires. It is in our power to change our beliefs and, in turn, change our reality.

What is a Belief

If you consider of reality and your beliefs as being static, then they lack the inherent adaptability that will let you alter your beliefs. Viewing beliefs and reality as fixed entities can hinder our ability to adapt and change. The potential for change is opened up by realising that beliefs are flexible constructs.

Unraveling the Essence of Beliefs:

Beliefs can be understood as thoughts that we consistently and repetitively engage with. Through this constant repetition, a powerful frequency is generated within the universe. It manifests as physical proof, thereby strengthening our beliefs. However, it is crucial to recognize that beliefs are not synonymous with objective truths or fixed realities. Instead, they are subjective interpretations of our experiences, offering us the best available explanation based on the evidence we have observed in our lives.

Imagine when you were a child, you had an experience where you enthusiastically shared an idea with a group of friends, but they reacted with laughter and made fun of you. In that moment, you might have felt embarrassed and thought, "I shouldn't speak up; people will just make fun of me."

As you continued to encounter situations where you felt hesitant to express yourself and got similar reactions, this initial meaning started to repeat itself. Over time, this pattern of feeling embarrassed and thinking that people might ridicule you could turn into a belief. You might begin to believe, "I'm not good enough to share my ideas; people will always make fun of me."

As this belief takes root, it starts influencing how you approach social situations. When you consider speaking up in a group, your belief might cause you to hesitate or avoid it altogether. Your belief is shaping your behavior based on the meaning you've assigned to past experiences.

What's important to note is that your belief isn't a fact; it's an interpretation you've developed over time. This belief about not being good enough is affecting your confidence and actions, even though the original events that led to it might have been isolated incidents.

This example illustrates how beliefs form: from initial meanings attached to experiences, to patterns that emerge from repeated situations, and finally to beliefs that influence how you perceive yourself and the world. Beliefs shape our behavior and emotions, showing that our interpretation of events plays a significant role in our overall experiences.

The key to personal growth lies in recognizing that beliefs can and should be subject to change, particularly when they hinder our progress rather than benefit us. Holding onto detrimental beliefs limits our potential and restricts our ability to embrace new possibilities. By questioning the validity and utility of our beliefs, we open the door to transformation and expansion.

To create a life that aligns with your aspirations, you will need careful evaluation of the beliefs. Beneficial beliefs are those that support your well-being, growth, and personal fulfilment. They are rooted in confidence, faith, trust, and acceptance. It is essential to cultivate beliefs that serve as empowering tools rather than self-imposed limitations. By consciously selecting beliefs that uplift and motivate us, we can shape a reality that reflects our desires and aspirations.

The Dynamic Nature of Reality:

Reality is not a fixed construct but a fluid and ever-evolving tapestry. Beliefs play a significant role in shaping our perception of reality. As we develop new insights and gather fresh evidence, our beliefs should evolve accordingly.

Imagine you're learning new things and discovering new evidence about the world. As you gather this new information, it's important to think about whether your beliefs still make sense or if they need to change to match the new things you're learning. Imagine you have a favorite pair of shoes that you love to wear all the time. But as you grow and your feet get bigger, those shoes might not fit as well anymore. Just like you would need new shoes that fit, our beliefs should also change and adapt as we learn and experience new things in life. Just as you wouldn't keep wearing the same shoes that are too small, we shouldn't hold onto beliefs that don't fit the evolving world around us.

Understanding that reality is always changing can help us handle the unpredictable twists and turns of life better. When we're open to considering new ideas and different ways of looking at things, we give ourselves the chance to keep growing and learning more about who we are and how the world works.

Changing a belief begins with self-reflection and awareness. We must examine the impact of our beliefs on our thoughts, emotions, and actions. If a belief proves detrimental, it is crucial to challenge it and seek alternative perspectives. Imagine your beliefs as the foundation for a building – if the foundation is weak or faulty, the whole building might be unstable. Similarly, if a belief is causing problems in our lives, it's important to question it and think about other ways to understand things.

This process might involve asking ourselves why we believe what we do and considering whether there are other perspectives or ideas we haven't thought about. Just like exploring new paths on a journey, we're exploring new ways of looking at the world. This might take time and effort, but it's worth it to have beliefs that help us feel better and make our lives better.

To have more positive beliefs, we need to trust ourselves and believe that we have the power to shape our own reality to some extent. It's like having confidence that you can paint your own picture on the ever-changing canvas of reality. This journey of changing beliefs and perspectives requires patience – like planting a seed and watching it grow – and it also takes determination to keep going, even when things get tough. It might mean trying out new ideas or stepping out of our comfort zones, but the result can be a richer, more fulfilling life as we learn and grow through the process.

Root (Core) Belief

When embarking on the journey of transforming our beliefs, it is essential to become aware of the core belief. This can be compared to exploring the depths of an ocean. Merely skimming the surface will not reveal the hidden wonders that lie beneath. Without diving deep, the true beauty remains undiscovered. Similarly, when addressing a belief, addressing surface-level thoughts, like "I am not talented enough," is like staying at the surface of the water. However, true transformation occurs when we plunge into the depths and examine the core belief, such as "I am unworthy of success," which holds the key to unlocking our potential.

Just like resilient plants that can resprout if their roots are left untouched, our beliefs can persist if their foundational core is not addressed. The thoughts we experience are like the visible branches of a plant—they are the result of a deeper-rooted belief system. To create lasting change, we must venture beneath the surface and confront the core belief that nurtures these limiting thoughts.

Imagine someone named Alex who has always felt like they're not good enough to pursue their dreams. This belief has been ingrained over the years due to various experiences and influences. At the surface level, Alex might think, "I don't have enough talent to succeed." However, this is just a branch of a deeper-rooted core belief that has shaped their self-perception.

The core belief for Alex might be something like, "I am unworthy of success." This belief acts as the foundation for their thoughts, feelings, and actions. It's like the roots of a plant that keep it growing in a certain way. Whenever Alex faces a challenge or an opportunity, this core belief influences how they approach it.

For instance, when Alex contemplates pursuing a new venture, their core belief might hold them back. Even if they try to dismiss the negative thoughts on the surface, the core belief keeps affecting their confidence and decisions. This core belief is powerful because it influences how Alex perceives themselves and the world around them.

To truly transform their beliefs, Alex needs to dive deep and confront this core belief head-on. By recognizing and challenging the belief that they are unworthy of success, they can start to change the way they see themselves and their potential. Over time, as Alex works on replacing this disempowering core belief with something like, "I am capable and deserving," they can reshape their reality and open themselves up to new possibilities.

LIGHT OF AWARENESS

BY SIMPLY BEING aware of our own beliefs, we initiate a process that loosens their grip on us. Identifying and examining our beliefs allows us to transcend their hold. It is important to recognize that the vibrational frequency of being immersed in a belief differs from that of observing it. When we truly believe we are not good enough, we are fully enveloped in that belief. However, when we shift our perspective and acknowledge it as a thought that has emerged, we step into the vibration of observation. This shift in vibration weakens the power of the belief, reducing its ability to manifest in our reality.

To embark on the journey of changing our beliefs, it is crucial to scrutinize the beliefs we hold, particularly the negative ones. We must remember that we have the right to question and consciously choose our beliefs. Beliefs that are acquired by default or influenced solely by external experiences are non-deliberate beliefs. It is essential to deliberately select the beliefs we hold, freeing ourselves from blindly accepting them as truth.

In order to transform our beliefs, we must detach ourselves from the notion of an absolute truth that exists independently of our perception. We need to let go of the idea that there is an ultimate truth that we must conform to. Justifying our beliefs based on an external truth only serves to limit our personal growth and autonomy. Instead, we should empower ourselves to consciously choose the beliefs that align with our authentic selves and desired reality.

Transcending the Illusion of Truth:

The key to changing beliefs lies in recognizing that truth is subjective and individual. There is no universal truth that dictates what we should believe. When we relinquish the notion of an external truth, we open ourselves up to the freedom of personal exploration and self-discovery. Each person holds the power to define their own truth, making choices based on their unique experiences, values, and aspirations.

To liberate ourselves from limiting beliefs, we must engage in a transformative process. This involves questioning the beliefs we hold and examining their origins, validity, and alignment with our true selves. It requires a willingness to explore alternative perspectives and challenge deeply ingrained notions. By consciously choosing our beliefs, we take ownership of our lives and actively shape our reality.

Changing our beliefs demands a sense of personal responsibility. We cannot rely on external sources or circumstances to dictate our beliefs. Instead, we must take proactive steps to evaluate and reshape our belief system. This might involve seeking knowledge, engaging in introspection, and seeking support from mentors, therapists, or coaches. By taking charge of our beliefs, we empower ourselves to create a life that aligns with our aspirations and values.

Unveiling Authenticity:

As we release the notion of an external truth and embrace personal choice, we uncover our authentic selves. By consciously choosing our beliefs, we align with our true desires, passions, and potentials. This alignment propels us towards a more fulfilling and meaningful existence. Embracing our individual truths allows us to embrace our uniqueness and live in harmony with our deepest aspirations.

By examining and questioning the beliefs we hold, we reclaim our power to choose beliefs that resonate with our authentic selves. This liberating process enables us to transcend self-imposed limitations and create a reality aligned with our true desires.

How To Find A Core Belief

We are creating our collective reality as well as our lives with the thoughts that we think every single day. Even if you don't believe that your thoughts literally weave the fabric of our reality, it's undeniable that the thoughts that we think dictate the decisions we make and that the decisions that we make plot the course of our entirelives. So it's quite evident,

How living a happy life really does depend upon findingthese thoughts and beliefs that are painful and changing them. There are beliefs that we could call surface beliefs. Beliefs such as "success is only for the lucky", "change is always difficult", or "expressing emotions is a sign of weakness". These thoughts resemble the branches of a tree, representing external manifestations of a more profound core belief.

The core belief is like the sturdy root of a towering tree. It serves as the fundamental building block of the life we lead. From this core belief, everything else branches out and grows. It shapes our perception of ourselves and influences how we perceive the universe we inhabit. Our core beliefs are not just abstract ideas; they have a tangible impact on our experiences.

These beliefs act as the deep-seated source of both joy and suffering in our lives. They can be the driving force behind our happiness and fulfillment, or they can become the barriers that hold us back. For instance, if someone holds the core belief of "I am unlovable," it can hinder their ability to form meaningful connections and experience love fully. Similarly, if a person carries the belief of "I will be hurt if I get close to someone," it can lead to emotional distance and prevent them from forming close bonds with others.

Core beliefs can be positive or negative, but for the sake of this discussion, let's focus on negative core beliefs because they are the ones that are not working for us. Core beliefs are mostly subconscious. They are the result of impactful experiences that we had in our childhoods. More often than not, core beliefs are the result of repeated experiences that are similar when we encounter certain situations.

As we go through these experiences, core beliefs take root and become deeply ingrained. They become inflexible and influence our perception of ourselves and the world around us. Paradoxically, we tend to ignore anything that challenges or invalidates these core beliefs while actively seeking evidence that supports them. This creates a never-ending cycle where our beliefs become reinforced, further solidifying their grip on our lives.

These core beliefs, once formed, become deeply embedded in our subconscious mind. They become a part of our human shadow—a term coined by Carl Jung to describe the unconscious aspects of our personality. Due to their subconscious nature, we are often unaware of these core beliefs, and yet, they silently shape our thoughts, emotions, and behaviors. Uncovering and transforming these core beliefs is a crucial part of shadow work—an inner journey of self-discovery and integration.

In order to beginthis journey of transformation, we must first become aware of the things that trigger us or cause emotional turmoil. Recognizing the thoughts and emotions that trigger us is a key step in this process. When we find ourselves feeling upset, anxious, or limited in any way, it presents an opportunity to explore the underlying core beliefs driving those emotions.

When experiencing an emotional turmoil, we can begin the process of actively and consciously questioning our thoughts and emotions. Two key questions come into play:

"Is it true?" and

"What meaning I assign to it?"

One effective way to uncover and challenge core beliefs is through a process of self-inquiry. By actively questioning our thoughts and emotions, we can unravel the layers of belief that underpin them. For example, let's consider the core belief "I am unlovable." By asking ourselves, "Is it true?" and if answer is yes "What meaning I assign to it" we might discover the answer, "It means I will always be alone." Continuing the inquiry, we ask, "Is it true?, What meaning I assign to it?" and uncover, "It means I am unworthy of love and connection." Digging deeper, we inquire, "Is it true?, What meaning I assign to it?" and realize, "It means I am fundamentally flawed." Through this process, we gradually unveil the core belief and the subsequent layers of beliefs connected to it.

1.Example Scenario: Receiving Criticism at Work:

Let's consider a different scenario where receiving criticism at work bothers you. We will explore the core belief finding process using this situation as an example.

Statement: "My colleague criticized my work."

Question 1: "Is it true?" if yes, "What meaning I assign to it?"

Response 1: "It means I'm not good enough at my job."

Question 2: "Is it true?" if yes, "What meaning I assign to it?"

Response 2: "I will never succeed in my career."

Question 3: “Is it true?” if yes, “What meaning I assign to it?"

Response 3: "I am a failure and incapable of achieving my goals."

Question 4: “Is it true?” if yes, “What meaning I assign to it?"

Response 4: "I will never be respected or valued by my colleagues."

Question 5: “Is it true?” if yes, “What meaning I assign to it?"

Response 5: "I am unworthy of success and recognition."

In this example, the core belief that emerges is "I am unworthy of success and recognition." It is triggered by the criticism received at work and reflects a deep-seated belief about one's self-worth and capabilities.

2.Example Scenario: Receiving Rejection in a Romantic Relationship:

Let's consider a different scenario where experiencing rejection in a romantic relationship triggers a sense of discomfort.

Statement: "My partner broke up with me."

Question 1: “Is it true?” if yes, “What meaning I assign to it?"

Response 1: "It means I am not lovable or worthy of love."

Question 2: “Is it true?” if yes, “What meaning I assign to it?"

Response 2: "I will always be alone and never find true love."

Question 3: “Is it true?” if yes, “What meaning I assign to it?"

Response 3: "I am fundamentally flawed and undeserving of happiness."

Question 4”Is it true?” if yes Or, “What meaning I assign to it?"

Response 4: "I will never be able to maintain a successful and fulfilling relationship."

Question 5: “Is it true?” if yes, “What meaning I assign to it?"
Response 5: "I am destined to be alone and unhappy in love."

In this example, the core belief that emerges is "I am destined to be alone and unhappy in love." It is triggered by the experience of rejection and reflects a deep-seated belief about one's worthiness and potential for love.

3.Example Scenario: Facing a Career Setback:

Let's consider a different example scenario where facing a significant career setback triggers internal turmoil.

Statement: "I was passed over for a promotion I had worked hard for."

Question 1: “Is it true?” if yes, “What meaning I assign to it?"

Response 1: "It means I am not valued or recognized for my efforts and contributions."

Question 2: “Is it true?” if yes, “What meaning I assign to it?"

Response 2: "I am a failure and incapable of achieving success in my career."

Question 3: “Is it true?” if yes, “What meaning I assign to it?"

Response 3: "I am not worthy of success"

Question 4: “Is it true?” if yes, “What meaning I assign to it?"

Response 4: "I feel unseen and un heard"

Question 5: “Is it true?” if yes, “What meaning I assign to it?"

Response 5: "I am un lovable"

In this example, the core belief that emerges is "I am un lovable" It is triggered by the experience of a career setback and reflects a deep-seated belief about one's self-worth and prospects for success.

JUSTIFICATIONS AND AVOIDING SHADOWS

WHEN YOU'RE IN THE process of discovering your core beliefs, you need to be cautious of justifications. Justifications are excuses we make to avoid confronting our deeper issues and shadows. For example, imagine you feel intense emotion because of you friend has ditched you on last minute for a plan, then you ask yourself, "What meaning I assign to it?" Then you might justify it by saying, "Because it makes me feel like people don't care." However, that's just a way of evading the true underlying fear. The real reason might be something like, "If they don't care about me, I feel completely alone." It's important to recognize when we're using justifications and instead explore the genuine reasons behind our feelings.

You can apply the process of questioning to any thought or judgment you possess, and you'll be amazed at the core beliefs you uncover. It's essential to understand that when you start this journey, you might discover multiple core beliefs. Identifying core beliefs can be challenging because they reside deep within our subconscious. When we bring them into conscious awareness, they might initially appear absurd or incredibly impactful at a fundamental level of our being.

In some instances, you may encounter more than one core belief during these exercises. These core beliefs are definitive statements about your life or yourself. It's crucial to work on all of these beliefs, not just the one that appears to be the core belief. Sometimes, we have a tendency to think, "That's it! I've reached the deepest level," but it's important to push further. Stopping prematurely often leads to circular thinking. For instance, in the scenario mentioned earlier, you need to question not only the belief that says, " people don't care" but also the belief that says, "I am not worthy." By exploring these beliefs more deeply, you'll gain a better understanding of their impact on your life.

questioning your beliefs is one powerful method. I highly recommend exploring this process and applying it to your core beliefs. It provides a structured approach to challenging and reframing your beliefs, leading to transformation. Once you've questioned your beliefs, it's time to initiate change. It's essential to consciously challenge these beliefs and actively search for evidence that contradicts their validity.

Additionally, these core beliefs can serve as a compass for determining what you'd rather believe. Once you've identified your core belief, ask yourself, "What would I prefer to believe instead?" This opens the door to new possibilities. Start seeking out proof that supports this new belief. Explore books, videos, and other resources that align with your desired belief. As you go about your daily life, continually ask yourself, "What actions would I take right now if I genuinely embraced this new belief with all my heart?" Then, take steps in alignment with that belief.

Remember, this journey of exploring and transforming your core beliefs can be life-changing. By delving deep into your thoughts, challenging justifications, and actively seeking new empowering beliefs, you'll unlock your inner strength and create a life of authenticity and fulfillment. Embrace the process with curiosity and openness, and you'll embark on a path of personal growth and self-discovery.

How to change a belief

The traditional approach to affirmations may not always yield the desired results for individuals. This is particularly true when people hold deeply ingrained beliefs, such as "I'm not good enough," which have been reinforced over the course of many years. Simply stating the opposite, such as "I am good enough," can trigger an emotional resistance because it contradicts their long-standing self-perception and feels like a lie.

Bridge The Gap

Rather than attempting to bridge the entire gap between where individuals currently perceive themselves and where they want to be, it is more effective to take incremental steps and create a series of stepping stones on the path of self-improvement.

Let's consider an example. Instead of using the affirmation "I am successful," which might feel distant or unattainable, individuals can choose a thought that aligns more closely with their current circumstances and still propels them forward. For instance, they can affirm, "I am making progress every day." If this thought resonates with their genuine belief and represents a step in the direction of success, it becomes a more empowering affirmation.

Here are a few more examples of affirmations that bridge the gap between self-doubt and self-assurance:

"I am continuously learning and growing." This affirmation recognizes the journey of personal development and emphasizes the value of ongoing improvement and expansion. It instills a sense of optimism and openness to new experiences.

"I am capable of overcoming challenges." This affirmation acknowledges that obstacles are part of life but affirms one's inner strength and resilience to face and conquer them. It promotes a mindset of determination and per severance."I am embracing my unique journey." This affirmation celebrates individuality and encourages self-acceptance. It emphasizes that everyone has their own path and that embracing one's unique qualities and experiences is a source of strength and authenticity.

"I am making progress every day." This affirmation recognizes that personal growth is a continuous journey. It emphasizes the importance of taking small steps forward, celebrating achievements along the way, and acknowledging that improvement is happening, even if it may not be apparent at first.

"I am capable of learning and adapting." This affirmation highlights individuals' inherent capacity to acquire new skills, expand their knowledge, and adapt to different situations. It encourages a growth mindset, emphasizing that capabilities can be developed with effort and practice.

By incorporating these incremental affirmations into daily practice, individuals gradually shift their beliefs and self-perception. As they consistently reinforce thoughts that align with their authentic truth and bring them closer to the vibration of their desired reality the gap between their current state and desired state begins to diminish.

Role of Affirmation, Proof and Belief

The concept of affirmation is not new; people have been using affirmations for years as a way to improve their performance and enhance their self-esteem. An affirmation is a positive statement that describes the way you want to be, and it focuses on a specific aspect of your performance that you want to achieve. Affirmations can help you to underpin your emotional management, and they should be personal, specific, positive, in the present tense, and use hot words.

Affirmations are powerful because they help to reprogram your subconscious mind. Your subconscious mind is the part of your mind that controls your beliefs, habits, and emotions, and it can be difficult to change. However, by repeating affirmations, you can start to reprogram your subconscious mind and change your beliefs, habits, and emotions.

Once you've identified your limiting beliefs, create positive affirmations that counteract those beliefs. Your affirmations should be positive, present tense, and focused on what you want to achieve. For example, if your limiting belief is "I'm not good enough," your affirmation could be "I am worthy and capable." To create your affirmations, you need to focus on specific qualities that you want to develop. For example, if you want to be more confident, your affirmation might be "I am a confident person." It is important to use positive language and focus on what you want to achieve, rather than what you don't want. You should also use hot words, which are words that have action and emotions that are meaningful to you.

Examples of Affirmations:

Here are some examples of positive affirmations that you could consider using:

"I am self-disciplined."

"I am emotionally strong."

"I am intellectually able."

"I communicate effectively, verbally and in writing, and I present well."

"I am good at interacting with others, and I am an effective team member."

"I build healthy, authentic relationships with other people."

"I am a good role model for others."

"I am a happy person, and I am able to express my happiness well."

"I am confident and successful in all areas of my life."

"I am worthy of love and respect."

"I am capable of achieving my goals and dreams."

"I am healthy and strong in body, mind, and spirit."

"I am grateful for all the blessings in my life."

Below are a few examples of negative affirmations and how you can use positive ones's to replace it.

Negative affirmation: "I am not good enough."

Positive affirmation: "I am worthy and capable."

Negative affirmation: "I can't do this."

Positive affirmation: "I am capable of achieving my goals."

Negative affirmation: "I am always so stressed out."

Positive affirmation: "I am calm and relaxed."

Negative affirmation: "I never have enough time."

Positive affirmation: "I have all the time I need to accomplish my goals."

Negative affirmation: "I am so unhappy."

Positive affirmation: "I am grateful for all the blessings in my life."

Negative affirmation: "I am so bad at making decisions."

Positive affirmation: "I trust myself to make the best decisions for me.

Negative affirmation: "I will never find love."

Positive affirmation: "I am deserving of love and will attract the right person for me."

Negative affirmation: "I can't lose weight."

Positive affirmation: "I am committed to my health and making healthy choices."

Top of Form

Repeat your affirmations daily: The key to using affirmations to change your beliefs is repetition. Repeat your affirmations daily, preferably multiple times a day. Say them out loud or silently to yourself, whichever feels more comfortable. For example, you may choose to repeat your affirmations first thing in the morning, before you go to bed, or throughout the day whenever you need a boo

Visualize your affirmations: As you repeat your affirmations, visualize yourself embodying those beliefs. Imagine yourself feeling confident, capable, and worthy. This visualization will help reinforce your affirmations and make them more effective. For example, if your affirmation is "I am successful in all areas of my life," imagine yourself achieving your goals, receiving recognition and praise, and feeling a sense of fulfillment and happiness.

Role of Confirmations On Belief

Affirmations are powerful tools for transforming our beliefs and shaping our reality. However, to maximize their effectiveness, it is important to back them up with confirmations. Confirmations provide concrete proof to our minds, helping us accept and integrate new ideas more readily.

Confirmations serve as evidence that supports the reality we are affirming. They act as building blocks for our belief system, gradually reinforcing our desired outcomes. When we consciously seek and acknowledge instances that align with our affirmations, we provide our minds with the necessary proof to solidify our new beliefs. This process helps us establish a deep sense of conviction and empowers our affirmations to manifest into reality.

Examples of Confirmations in Practice:

Confidence Confirmation:

Suppose you are affirming, "I am confident in all areas of my life." Throughout the day, pay attention to moments when you genuinely felt confident. It could be successfully delivering a presentation, engaging in a difficult conversation with ease, or stepping out of your comfort zone to try something new. By consciously recognizing and celebrating these instances of confidence, you reinforce your affirmation and build a stronger belief in your inherent confidence.

Achievement Confirmation:

Let's say your affirmation is, "I effortlessly achieve my goals." Notice and appreciate even the smallest achievements in your daily life. It could be completing a task ahead of schedule, receiving positive feedback from a colleague, or reaching a personal milestone. By acknowledging and celebrating these accomplishments, you provide your mind with evidence that affirms your ability to achieve your desired outcomes effortlessly.

Abundance Confirmation:

If your affirmation is focused on abundance, such as "I attract abundance in all areas of my life," look for signs of abundance around you. It could be receiving unexpected gifts, opportunities, or experiencing moments of financial abundance. By actively seeking and acknowledging these instances, you strengthen your belief in the abundance that already exists in your life and open yourself to attracting more of it.

Health and Well-being Confirmation:

Suppose you are affirming, "I am healthy and vibrant." Pay attention to moments when you experience vitality, energy, and overall well-being. It could be participating in physical activities, feeling a sense of inner peace, or experiencing improvements in your overall health. By intentionally recognizing and appreciating these moments, you reinforce your affirmation and nurture a stronger belief in your own health and vitality.

Relationship Confirmation:

If your affirmation focuses on relationships, such as "I attract loving and harmonious connections," notice instances of positive interactions with others. It could be receiving heartfelt compliments, experiencing deep and meaningful conversations, or feeling supported and loved by your loved ones. By consciously acknowledging these moments of connection, you reinforce your belief in attracting loving relationships into your life.

Why use confirmations?

By incorporating confirmations into your practice of affirmations, you can enhance the effectiveness of your transformational journey. Confirmations provide tangible evidence that reinforces your new beliefs, creating a stronger foundation for positive change.By actively seeking and acknowledging confirmations, you can develop a deep sense of conviction in the validity of your affirmations, empowering them to manifest more readily. The practice of seeking confirmations cultivates a heightened state of awareness, allowing you to recognize and appreciate positive experiences more readily. you shift your attention towards the positive aspects of your life, fostering a mindset of gratitude

Stepping into Your Power

Observing the behaviors of individuals around us, we often witness a common pattern: people who consistently complain about their lives. It is disheartening to see how these individuals unknowingly hold themselves back due to their deeply ingrained beliefs about themselves and their circumstances. What is even more troubling is their reluctance to take responsibility for their lives. In many cases, they are simply unaware of what is truly shaping the reality they experience. This lack of awareness stems from a misconception that reality is fixed and beyond their influence.

The prevailing belief is that individuals exist as passive participants in the fabric of reality, susceptible to the whims of fate. They assume that negative events can occur randomly, without any invitation or intentional focus on their part. However, this perspective is inherently flawed. The universe is designed to operate as a reflection of our thoughts and beliefs. Our inner world, consisting of our conscious and subconscious thoughts, plays a pivotal role in shaping the external reality we experience.

If one finds themselves leading a life that falls short of being satisfactory and joyful, it is important to recognize that their focus, thoughts, and beliefs are not aligned with their true desires. These aspects of their inner world are out of sync with their authentic selves and the thoughts that evoke positive emotions. To bring about a different life experience, in any aspect or area, it is imperative to change the narrative we tell ourselves about our lives.

This transformation begins by deliberately altering the thoughts we choose to entertain and cultivate. When we consciously shift our thought patterns, it sets in motion a profound change in the way our reality structures itself. Consequently, our beliefs about reality undergo a fundamental shift as well. As this inner transformation unfolds, others around us may be astounded by the remarkable life we have created for ourselves—a life characterized by boundless bliss and freedom.

In those moments of amazement, we can confidently say that the change in our reality was made possible because we took the initiative to change our daily thoughts and beliefs. By consciously and intentionally shifting our mindset, we set in motion a cascade of transformative events that aligned our reality with our deepest desires. Through our deliberate efforts, we became the architects of our own reality.

It is important to emphasize that this transformative process is not limited to a select few; it is available to each and every one of us. The potential for change exists within the space we currently occupy, as our focus of power lies within ourselves. With unwavering determination and a willingness to challenge our existing beliefs, we can embark on a profound journey of self-discovery and personal empowerment.

In closing, I hope this expanded perspective provides valuable insights as you navigate through your life. May it serve as a reminder of your innate ability to shape your own reality and inspire you to take control of your thoughts and beliefs. By doing so, you can manifest a life filled with limitless joy and fulfilment.